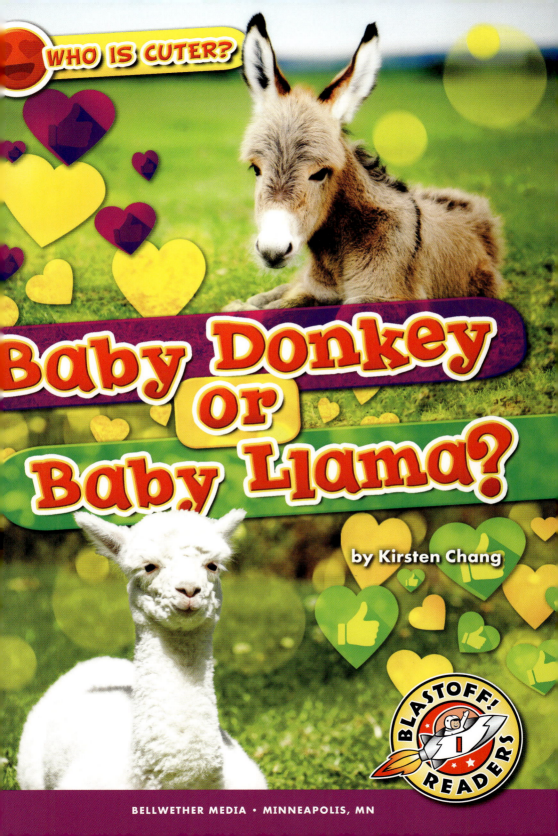

Blastoff! Readers are carefully developed by literacy experts to build reading stamina and move students toward fluency by combining standards-based content with developmentally appropriate text.

Level 1 provides the most support through repetition of high-frequency words, light text, predictable sentence patterns, and strong visual support.

Level 2 offers early readers a bit more challenge through varied sentences, increased text load, and text-supportive special features.

Level 3 advances early-fluent readers toward fluency through increased text load, less reliance on photos, advancing concepts, longer sentences, and more complex special features.

★ **Blastoff! Universe**

This edition first published in 2025 by Bellwether Media, Inc.

No part of this publication may be reproduced in whole or in part without written permission of the publisher. For information regarding permission, write to Bellwether Media, Inc., Attention: Permissions Department, 6012 Blue Circle Drive, Minnetonka, MN 55343.

Library of Congress Cataloging-in-Publication Data

Names: Chang, Kirsten, 1991- author.
Title: Baby donkey or baby llama? / by Kirsten Chang.
Description: Minneapolis, MN : Bellwether Media, Inc., 2025. | Series: Blastoff! Readers: who is cuter? | Includes bibliographical references and index. | Audience term: Children | Audience term: School children | Audience: Ages 5-8 | Audience: Grades K-1 | Summary: "Developed by literacy experts for students in kindergarten through grade three, this book introduces baby donkey or baby llama to young readers through leveled text and related photos"–Provided by publisher
Identifiers: LCCN 2024035016 (print) | LCCN 2024035017 (ebook) | ISBN 9798893042245 (library binding) | ISBN 9798893044034 (paperback) | ISBN 9798893043211 (ebook)
Subjects: LCSH: Donkeys–Infancy–Juvenile literature. | Llamas–Infancy–Juvenile literature.
Classification: LCC QL706.2 .C44 2025 (print) | LCC QL706.2 (ebook) | DDC 599.13/92–dc23/eng/20240814
LC record available at https://lccn.loc.gov/2024035016
LC ebook record available at https://lccn.loc.gov/2024035017

Text copyright © 2025 by Bellwether Media, Inc. BLASTOFF! READERS and associated logos are trademarks and/or registered trademarks of Bellwether Media, Inc.

Editor: Rachael Barnes   Designer: Brittany McIntosh

Table of Contents

Foals and Crias!	4
Short and Tall	8
Bray and Hum	14
Who Is Cuter?	20
Glossary	22
To Learn More	23
Index	24

Foals and Crias!

Baby donkeys are called foals. Baby llamas are crias.

These cute babies have thick **coats**. They both have big ears.

thick coat

Short and Tall

Foals walk on **hooves**. Crias have big nails.

big nails

hooves

Both babies must reach the ground to **graze**. Foals have short legs. Crias bend long necks.

Both babies have fluffy tails. Foals have longer tails than crias.

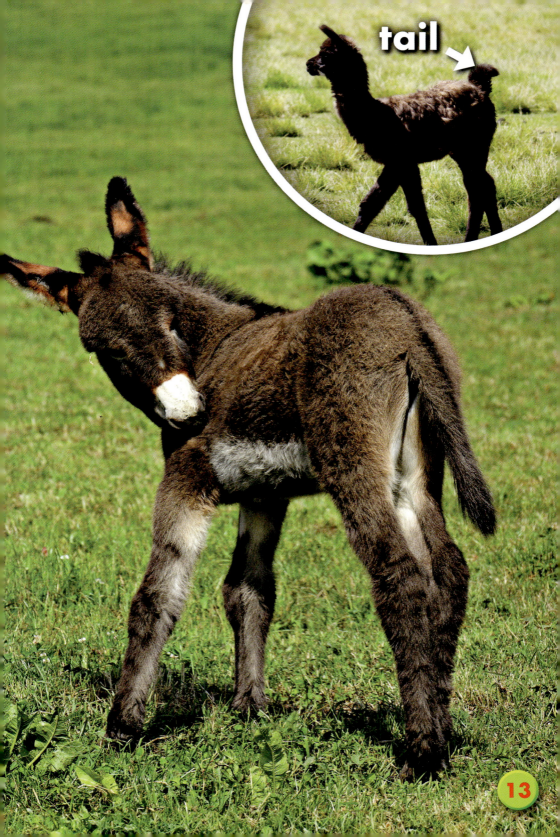
tail

Bray and Hum

Foals live in **droves**.
Crias live in **herds**.
Both babies
stay close to mom.

Both babies are noisy! Foals can **bray**. Crias hum.

Foals play tag. Crias run and jump to play. Which is cuter?

playing

Who Is Cuter?

long, fluffy tail

short legs

hooves

Baby Donkey

lives in a drove

plays tag

Glossary

bray
to make a loud sound

graze
to feed on grasses

coats
the hair or fur covering some animals

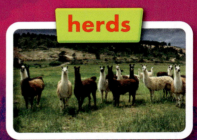
herds
groups of llamas that live together

droves
groups of donkeys

hooves
hard coverings on the feet of donkeys

To Learn More

AT THE LIBRARY

Bodden, Valerie. *Llamas*. Mankato, Minn.: Creative Education and Creative Paperbacks, 2023.

Hinman, Bonnie. *Farm Animals*. Minneapolis, Minn.: Abdo Publishing, 2023.

Leaf, Christina. *Baby Horse or Baby Cow?* Minneapolis, Minn.: Bellwether Media, 2025.

ON THE WEB

FACTSURFER

Factsurfer.com gives you a safe, fun way to find more information.

1. Go to www.factsurfer.com.

2. Enter "baby donkey or baby llama" into the search box and click 🔍.

3. Select your book cover to see a list of related content.

Index

bray, 16
coats, 6, 7
donkeys, 4
droves, 14
ears, 6
graze, 10, 11
herds, 14
hooves, 8, 9
hum, 16
legs, 10
llamas, 4
mom, 14
nails, 8, 9
necks, 10, 11
play, 18, 19
tails, 12, 13

The images in this book are reproduced through the courtesy of: miskokordic, front cover (donkey); Jiri Vondrous, front cover (llama); Lili Boyle, p. 3 (llama); Eric Isselee, pp. 3 (donkey), 20 (donkey); Jacques Durocher Photo, pp. 4-5; Edwin Remsberg/ Alamy, p. 5 (cria); Mira Amtmann, pp. 6-7; autbmoore, p. 7; Geza Farkas, pp. 8-9, 16-17, 19, 20 (lives in droves); Dudarev Mikhail, p. 9 (big nails); Stock video footage, pp. 10-11; Lars Christensen/ Alamy, p. 11 (grazing); Marie Charouzova, pp. 12-13; Stefano Paterna/ Alamy, p. 13 (tail); Jeff McCollough, pp. 14-15; blickwinkel/ Alamy, p. 15; Chris Howarth/Bolivia/ Alamy, p. 17 (hum); Omar_87, pp. 18-19; Manfred Grebler/ Alamy, p. 20 (plays tag); photomaster, p. 21 (llama); Nik Taylor Wildlife/ Alamy, p. 21 (lives in herds); Budimir Jevtic, p. 21 (runs and jumps); MrAli00, p. 22 (bray); SERSOLL, p. 22 (coats); Vera Larina, p. 22 (droves); vito natale, p. 22 (graze); Josh Cornish, p. 22 (herds); Chris Howes/Wild Places Photography/ Alamy, p. 22 (hooves).